The Pilgrimage of Life and the Wisdom of Rumi

Poems and Translations

by

Seyyed Hossein Nasr

The Pilgrimage of Life and the Wisdom of Rumi

Published by **The Foundation for Traditional Studies**

The calligraphy of the Persian poems appearing on pages 22, 28, 40, 50, and 59 is by the contemporary Persian calligrapher Leila Kokabi.

Printed in the United States of America

ISBN 0962998451

The Foundation for Traditional Studies
P.O. Box 370
Oakton, VA 22124
www.ftsdc.org

Table of Contents

Part II: A Few Moments with Rumi

بسم الله الرحمن الرحيم

Lighting the Guiding Lamp for the Lovers of Layla: The Mystical Path of Seyyed Hossein Nasr

"The Inner Journey above the heavens resides..."
—Seyyed Hossein Nasr

With this second volume of poetry, Seyyed Hossein Nasr, whose name the reader usually associates with the philosopher, the historian and the scientist, firmly establishes his role as a spiritual mentor of the highest rank. In *The Pilgrimage of Life and the Wisdom of Rumi*, as in his former *Poems of the Way*,[1] the poet further explores the pilgrimage of life and invites us to realize what our true transcendent destination really is. This time, however, Nasr's poetical rendering of the Way uncovers increasingly deeper spiritual secrets: so much so that his allegorical pilgrimage turns into a veritable mystical path. It is no wonder that the poet chooses to address in his verses precisely his "friends of the Path" (p. 24), who are none other than the "lovers of Layla" (p. 23): those enamored by the infinite darkness of the One, Who seems dark because of the overwhelming abundance of His radiance.

Many gnostics have walked before the strenuous path from the Alpha to the Omega of life and thus have "lighted the guiding lamp" (p. 51) for future generations. We have countless examples of their symbolic spiritual journeys in both the Christian and the Islamic spiritual traditions, and it is evident that Seyyed Hossein Nasr follows these daring travelers of the profound recesses of the soul in this second poetical rendition of his personal path.

---

[1] Published by the Foundation for Traditional Studies (Oakton, Virginia, 1999), and translated into Spanish by L. López-Baralt as *Poemas de la vía mística* (Mandala Ediciones: Madrid, 2002).

The traditional *leitmotif* of the *homo viator* has an exterior, historic manifestation in the religious pilgrimages to the holy city of Mecca, to Jerusalem or to Santiago de Compostela. But we must keep in mind that all these venerable voyages have as their true *desideratum* a profound spiritual transformation. As Leonard J. Bowman[2] points out, the spiritual travelers bear witness with their pilgrimage that no city on earth is safe nor stable, so they struggle to reach instead the Immutable Celestial City within their souls. The outward pilgrimage always implies an interior spiritual process, a personal eschatological journey. St. Augustine's *Confessions* and St. Bonaventure's *Itinerarium* were pioneer texts in this symbolic odyssey of the soul.[3] Dante follows suit with the *peregrinatio animae* of his *Divine Comedy*, which is, much like Raimundo Lulio's *Blanquerna,*[4] heavily indebted to Islamic eschatological legends.[5] Even the symbolic quest of the Holy Grail depicted in the early medieval novels of chivalry of the Arthurian cycle is but an allegory of the quest for the Invisible. The secret sub-text of the novels is, in the end, Augustinian: *in interiore hominis habitat veritas.*[6]

The Persian Sufis, followers of both Plato and Zoroaster, show particular sophistication and insight in their treatment of their autobiographical *itinerarium sacri amoris*. We are indebted to Shihābuddīn Yahyā Suhrawardī for several treatises describing the mystical itinerary of the soul: the *Hikmāt al-ishrāq* ("The Philosophy of Illumination"), the *Hayākil al-nūr* ("The Altars of Light") and the *'Aql-e Sorkh* ("The Red Intellect"). In the case of gnostic narratives such as these, the path of the soul towards itself takes the weary traveler through dangerous

[2] "*Itinerarium*: the Shape of a Metaphor," in: L. Bowman, ed., *Itinerarium: the Idea of Journey* (Institut für Anglistik und Amerikanistik Universität Salzburg: Salzburg, 1983), p. 10.

[3] Cf.. Robert O'Connell, *St. Augustine's Confessions: the Odyssey of Soul* (Harvard University Press: Cambridge, 1969).

[4] Cf. Lina Cofresi, "*Itinerarium sacri amoris*: The Road to God in Ramon Lull's *Blanquerna*", in: L. Bowman, op. cit., pp. 170-177.

[5] Miguel Asín Palacios demonstrated it long ago in his *La escatología musulmana de la Divina comedia* (Instituto Hispano-Arabe de Cultura: Madrid, 1961).

[6] The inner spiritual meaning of these novels of chivalry has been studied in depth: cf. as representative examples the essays of John Matthews, *The Mystic Grail: the Challenge of the Arthurian Quest* (Thorsens: London, 1997), and of Bernard Levy, "Gawain's Spiritual Journey: *Imitatio Christi* in Sir Gawain and the Green Knight" (*Annuale Medievale* VI, 1965, pp. 65-106).

adventures and strange imaginal *loci*, which Henry Corbin has explored in depth.[7]

But these "Inner guides to the One" (p. 54)[8] also know that the interior pilgrimage is particularly difficult because it implies a courageous *jihād* or holy war against the lower soul or *nafs*. The *homo viator* turns into a spiritual *chevalier* as he fights this awesome war from within the ramparts of the fortified castle of his innermost heart. Al-Hujwirī describes the struggle in vivid allegorical terms:

> The Apostle said: "We have returned from the lesser war *(al-jihād al-asghar)* to the greatest war (*al-jihād al-akbar*)." What is the greatest war? He replied, "It is the struggle against one's self (*mujāhadat al-nafs*)."[9]

We are dealing here with the metaphor of the *javānmardī*, "*c'est-à dire de 'chevalerie spirituelle'*," according to Henry Corbin.[10] Most Sufis are quite familiar with the simile: Al-Ghazālī (*Ihyā' 'ulūm al-dīn*), al-Kubrā (*Fawā'ih al-jamāl*), Ibn 'Arabī (*Tarjumān al-ashwāq*), Ibn 'Atā' Allāh (*Kitāb-al-tanwīr fī isqāt al-tadbīr*).[11] Again, this *leitmotif* of the spiritual warrior within the fortified citadel of the soul belongs to a renowned literary tradition in both the East and the West. We are indebted to the Pseudo-Dionysius' *Celestial Hierarchies* for one of the earliest literary depictions of this symbolic warfare, which Portuguese and especially Spanish contemplatives went on to elaborate in minute detail. Again, it must be said that some of them—Raimundo Lulio,[12]

---

[7] Cf. Henry Corbin essays: *L'Archange empourprée* (Fayard: Paris, 1978); *L'Imagination Créatrice dans le soufisme d'Ibn 'Arabi* (Flammarion: Paris, 1975); and *L'homme de lumière dans le soufisme iranien* (Présence: Paris, 1961). For the Spanish version of these mystical pilgrimages, cf. LuceLópez-Baralt, *Asedios a lo Indecible: San Juan de la Cruz canta al éxtasis transformante* (Trotta: Madrid, 1998).

[8] I am quoting Nasr's *The Pilgrimage of Life*, and will indicate only the page number in the forthcoming quotes.

[9] *Kashf al-Mahjūb. The Oldest Persian Treatise in Sufism*, R.A. Nicholson, trad. (Gibb Memorial Series, vol. XVII: London, 1976), p. 12.

[10] *L'Homme de lumière dans le soufisme iranien*, op. cit., p. 12.

[11] Cf. Kamāl al-Dīn Husayn Kāshifī, *The Royal Book of Spiritual Chivalry: Futuwwat-Nāma-yi Sultānī*, (Great Books of the Islamic World, 2000).

[12] Cf. Mark Johnston, "Literacy, Spiritual Allegory and Power: Lull's *Libre de l'ordre de cavalleria*" (*Catalan Review International* IV, 1-2 (1990)), pp. 357-376.

Lourenzo Justiniano, Fray Luis de Granada, Fray Alonso de Madrid, Francisco de Osuna, St. Teresa of Avila, St. John of the Cross—seem to owe much to Sufis like Abū'l-Hasan al-Nūrī, Al-Hakīm al-Tirmidī and Muhammad ibn Mūsā al-Damīrī, who traveled before them through the seven castles of their inner souls.[13]

Seyyed Hossein Nasr's *The Pilgrimage of Life* is written in the same spirit of his venerable predecessors from both the Islamic and the Christian tradition. The Holy Quran is the poet's ultimate guide in his struggle to achieve the Way's Ultimate goal: "But those who struggle in Our cause, surely We shall guide them in Our ways" (XXIX, 69).[14] A veritable *mujāhid* or mystical warrior, the poet knows well that the holy war (or, better still, holy Endeavor) *fī sabī i'Llāh*—in the Path or Cause of God—is long and dangerous and that it must be fought during the whole span of one's life. So strenuous is this Path that mankind has strayed from it once and again: "We have now fallen and forgotten who we are, / wandering on earth with no compass in hand." (p. 29) *The Pilgrimage of Life* constitutes precisely this lost symbolic compass that the poet offers his fellow travelers along the Path.

Nasr explores the Way that must be trod as a symbolic Pilgrim from different angles. First, he gives a personal testimony of his intimate journey to the One, whose resplendent Countenance and Theophanic Presence is elaborated in inebriated verses. This inner spiritual process is later concretized into the symbolic pilgrimages to the holy sites of Islam (the Holy Mecca, Humaythara in Egypt, Marrakesh) which are reminders of the deeper personal path to the interior soul. At the end of the poetry collection the author has "A Few Moments with Rumi" and translates from the Persian some of the finest poems of the *Mathnawī* and the *Dīwān*. Nasr sustains an ardent dialogue with this foremost Sufi master, his countryman and his very special companion of the Path. Both mystical poets identify with the reed that narrates the poignant

---

[13] For the Sufi and Christian versions of the interior castles, cf. Miguel Asín Palacios, *Sadilíes y alumbrados* (Hiperión: Madrid, 1990) and L. López-Baralt "Teresa de Jesús y el Islam. El símil de los siete castillos concéntricos del alma" in: Pablo Beneito, ed., *Mujeres de luz* (Trotta: Madrid, 2001), pp. 53-76.

[14] All my quotes from the Quran come from Arthur Arberry's version, *The Koran Interpreted* (Oxford University Press: London, 1964). The Holy Quran also makes detailed reference to the rites of pilgrimage to the Ka'bah (the *Hajj*, the *'Umra*) in chapters II: 158, 196-203; III: 97 and XXII: 26-33.

tale of separation since both have had the heart-rending experience of feeling "cut from the reed-bed" (p. 73) of their true celestial origins.

But as I pointed out in the beginning, these poems do not simply rewrite the allegorical pilgrimage of the traditional *homo viator*. The epigraph of the book immediately suggests its most significant lesson, which is deeply mystical. Nasr purposely opens with Ibn 'Arabī's words:

> When my Beloved appears,
> With which eyes do I behold Her?[15]
> With Her eyes, not with mine.
> For no one sees Her but Herself see. (p. 17)

These sapient verses from the *Futūhāt* celebrate the supreme mystery of the *Unus/Ambo*: the illuminated mystic realizes that to attain direct knowledge of the Absolute he must first be "transformed" into that same Absolute. We are dealing here with *al-hikmat al-dhawqiyyah* or "tasted knowledge" of the Sacred, which always has been at the very center of Nasr's poetry. The soul and the One are melted into Unity when the obstacles for union are volatilized in this supreme moment beyond time. Frithjof Schuon, a contemporary mystical sage, describes the mysterious process with the intuition of a true rhapsodist:

> What separates man from divine Reality is the slightest of barriers. God is infinitely close to man, but man is infinitely far from God. The barrier, for man, is a mountain [...] which he must remove with his own hand. He digs away the earth, but in vain, the mountain remains; man goes on digging in the Name of God. And the mountain vanishes. It was never there.[16]

Like Schuon's symbolic mountain, the Alpha and Omega of life's pilgrimage is mercifully dissolved into Unity in Nasr's *The Pilgrimage of Life*. If this difficult path is trod correctly, the wary pilgrim discovers that the distance that separates him from his Transcendent goal is but

---

[15] As he did in his *Poems of the Way*, Nasr addresses God as a symbolic woman. For more on this traditional Sufi metaphor, cf. note 18.

[16] From *Stations of Wisdom*, in Laleh Bakhtiar, *Sufi. Expressions of the Mystic Quest* (Thames & Hudson: London, 1976), p. 57.

an illusion. Let us take a closer look at the spiritual lesson, unexpected because of its very depth, which underlies the poet's verses.

From the beginning, Nasr insists on the difficulties and dangers of the Path. We seem to be lost in a "centerless circle" (p. 46), and must "awaken unto the world of light from that murky existence, / that thy ego mistakes for reality". (p. 30) Constant awareness of our true "Origin and End" (p. 29) will have, however, dire consequences for our earthly journey: our pilgrimage will be suddenly transformed into an eschatological quest. The Alpha or beginning of this symbolic Way is no other than the Eternal Covenant mankind made with God in pre-eternity, bearing witness to His Lordship (Quran VII, 172). Nasr offers a poetical rendering of the Quranic verses as a spiritual warning for the *homo viator*:

> Let us not forget who we are, whence we came, where we shall go;
> Let us not forget that pre-eternal day when we bore witness,
> Bore witness to His Lordship with a resounding yea,
> Which does still echo under the vaults of the celestial realm.
>
> (p. 29)[17]

Nasr poses an awesome spiritual query surreptitiously, as merits a true poet: since the Alpha or origin of our Path is timeless, how can we reach the Omega without abolishing time itself? Traveling implies distance and time, but Nasr's fellow traveler is suddenly made aware that the true spiritual path from the symbolic Alpha to the Omega is trod, curiously enough, outside of time and space. As we shall soon see, this is precisely one of the poet's most significant mystical lessons.

Nasr continues to elaborate the drama of our celestial origin. In that pre-eternal dawn of our creation, God breathed the "nectar of grace" (p. 36) of His Spirit into the pure chalice of our souls. We have desecrated it (the body drags us to a "prison of water and clay" p. 95) and must again strive to become "that hallowed chalice here below". (p. 37) It is important to notice that the poet insists that the spiritual transformation must be achieved "here below"—the spell of our exile must be broken while still in the midst of this earthly pilgrimage which

[17] In Nasr's *Poems of the Way* the same idea is rendered in verse in "The Eternal Covenant" (op. cit., p. 20).

is, ironically, immersed in time. This, in spite of the fact that the poet repeats, on the other hand, a warning that seems to imply precisely the merciless cycle of change and transience: death draws near and might break unexpectedly the vessel of our souls. It is well known that Islamic lore depicts in fearsome detail the punishments of the tomb. Again the reader asks: how can death and time be conquered "here below"?

For the moment, the poet still dwells on his nostalgia for his lost blissful Alpha of origin, and his spiritual *saudade* is indeed overwhelming. His dire need for safety and tenderness is dramatized when he addresses God as a symbolical woman. Nasr's erotic similes might seem daring but are, again, typical of the Sufi mystical discourse. Many Muslim mystics like Ibn 'Arabī claim that God is better understood under His feminine aspect,[18] and our poet, just like his antecessors, cannot seem to forget "the Beloved's embrace, / the warmth of her bosom when we in union were". (p. 29)

But while celebrating the One for the "intimacy" of "Her Embrace", (p. 24) the poet also associates God with His mighty "resplendent Throne" (p. 25) or majestically alludes to Him as "The Alone". (p. 34) It is obvious that Nasr, as a true mystic, is employing here what Michael Sells calls the "language of unsaying"[19]: Gnostics know that God transcends language, so they annul any verbal affirmation of His Essence by words that "un-say" or contradict it. All mystical traditions make good use of this supremely knowledgeable *apophatic* language, for "the Tao that can be said is not the Tao". The repeated literary paradoxes of mystical discourse also imply that the soul is entering the blessed state of the *coincidentia oppositorum* or unitive knowledge, something that the rational mind can never apprehend. Nasr follows suit and paradoxically conceives the Transcendent, Almighty Creator as a delicate woman of indescribable beauty. Still more, he contemplates

---

[18] Ibn 'Arabī, among other Sufis, celebrated both God and the beautiful Nizām in his *Tarjumān al-ashwāq*. The Shaykh al-akbar understands that when man contemplates God in the form of a woman, he contemplates Him as both *agens* and *patiens*. From a feminine perspective, God is *agens* because he has total control over the soul of man, but is also *patiens* because women are under men's control. Cf. Annemarie Schimmel's *My Soul is a Woman. The Feminine in Islam.* (Continuum: New York, 1998, p. 102).

[19] *Mystical Languages of Unsaying* (The University of Chicago Press: Chicago-London, 1994), p. 9.

this radiant "Sun of all Suns" (p. 31) as Layla, the "beauty of the Night". (p. 23) Radiance and darkness joyfully coexist.

Layla (which in Arabic means precisely "night") is Majnūn's beloved, the heroine of a delicate Bedouin legend of chaste love. Pre-Islamic poets or *jāhiliyyūn* were the first to sing the famous story of this Romeo and Juliet of the East, and poets like Nizāmī, Fudūlī and even Clara Janés in contemporary Spain have continued to elaborate the legend. Qays, a poet from ancient Arabia, loved Layla, but her family opposed the wedding and married her off to a better suitor. Qays turns mad—*majnūn* means insane—and takes refuge in the desert, where he lives among the beasts and sings about his beloved in desperate verses. But in his solitude Majnūn makes a stunning discovery: he finds his lost Layla in his own heart. Once widowed, Layla returns to Majnūn, only to find that he does not need her any more, for he has already been transformed into her essence in his innermost soul.

Needless to say, Sufis took advantage of the chaste story of spiritual love for their own purposes, and thus the dark night of the soul became a recognizable *leitmotif* in the passionate works of mystics such as Shabistarī, Suhrawardī, Simnānī, and Niffarī. Rumi insists that the mystic must embrace this symbolic "Night" that leads to transformation in the One:

> Take the Leyla 'Night' [*leyl*] on your breast, o Majnun:
> The night is the secret chamber of *tawhid* [Unity],
> and the day idolatry (*sherk*) and multiplicity…"[20]

Nasr is part of this venerable mystical tradition and beholds the Transcendent beauty of Layla's face—"Thou art the Essence, darkness shining as the desert sun at noon" (p. 23)—and, like Rumi is "granted intimacy" (p. 24) in Her sacred Embrace. The journey back to The Sacred has begun for this foremost "lover of Layla", even in the midst of his earthly existence. Majnūn's beloved is immaterial, timeless, transcendent, and the Lover can only attain union with Her in the innermost heart.

[20] *Dīwān-e kabīr* 155/1773, in A. Schimmel, *The Triumphal Sun. A Study of the Works of Jalāloddin Rūmī* (East-West Publications: London and The Hague, 1980), p. 346.

The poet's spiritual pilgrimage takes another unsuspected turn when he arrives at what Sufis call the mystical station of proximity (*al-qurb*). The One whispers to his devoted lover, "I am Near", (Quran II, 186) but I dare to say that in poems like "The Luminous Wine of Gnosis", one of Nasr's most original and moving of the whole collection, He is verily "nearer to him than the jugular vein". (Quran L:15) The "desiccated landscape" (p. 31) of the poet's dry soul is transformed before our very eyes into Light as the poet drinks the supernatural Wine of Ecstasy. Again, the symbol of this mystical inebriation is typical of Sufi lore. Shabistarī exclaims in his *Wine of Rapture*:

> Drink this wine and, dying to self,
> You will be freed from the spell of self...
> What sweetness! What intoxication! What blissful ecstasy![21]

For Ibn 'Arabī, this symbolic intoxication represents the fourth highest level of God's manifestation, while for Simnānī this "sweet inebriation" corresponds to the number 87 of the ninth station of ecstasy.[22] A passionate Sufi, Nasr abandons sobriety (*sahw*) for intoxication (*sukr*) and slowly—yet surely—becomes a "man of light":

> As I drink this pure Wine, its heat warms my blood,
> Its light turns each of its drops into a particle of light,
> And the drops now luminous flow, guided to the heart,
> Finding their way to the Sun at the Center where Thou resideth,
> The Center which was always there, but I knew not.
> My body now luminous, I have become a man of light. (p. 31)

Immersed in the Uncreated Light, every particle of the poet's now luminous blood flows toward the One that he discovers in his interior soul. His whole being turned "into a ray of light", the poet can now be reabsorbed into the Ultimate "Sun of all Suns". "*Nūrun 'alā nūr*: Light upon Light; (God guides to His Light whom he will.)" (Quran XXIV; 35) In this incandescent, truly sapiental poem of "tasted knowledge",

---

[21] In Margaret Smith, *The Sufi Path of Love, An Anthology of Sufism* (Luzac & Co.: London, 1954), p. 113.

[22] Cf. the *Kashf al-Mahjub of Al-Hujwīrī. The Oldest Persian Treatise on Sufism*, p. 187.

Seyyed Hossein Nasr turns into an *illuminati*, a true *homme de lumière*. Again, he is updating the secret literary code of Sufism, for in the highly developed metaphysics of light of Islamic gnostics like Ibn 'Abād of Ronda, Abū'l-Hasan al-Shadhilī, Ibn 'Arabī, al-Kubrā, and especially Suhrawardī, considered as the Shaykh al-ishrāq, or "Master in the Philosophy of Illumination", being one of the *ishrāqīyyūn* or "enlightened" means that a very high spiritual station has been attained. In a poetic *tour de force*, Nasr masterfully makes simultaneous use of two different Sufi symbols to sing of his attainment of Unitive Knowledge.

Nasr's enlightened inebriation makes him exclaim in ecstasy: "O Sun residing at the Center of my heart" (p. 31) The Gnostic's supreme lesson is clear, for again the reader realizes in awe that the pilgrimage has definitely become an interior way. Where can the spiritual path lead him now but to himself? The poet has established joyous contact with his interior heart, which in Sufism is precisely the seat of Gnosis or *qalb*. There he has found the All: "the Source of my being, the Source of all that is". (p. 31) The timeless Alpha was within the soul all the time. The path leads to our very center and thus has to be traversed inwardly. That is exactly why "the inner journey above the heavens resides" (p. 85): distance has been abolished and the heresy of separation has ceased. The poet can claim, with mystics of every religious persuasion, that "I Myself the Beloved, am". (p. 67)

The poet is left gloriously "alone with the Alone" (p. 34) and continues to utter paradoxical verses in victorious bewilderment (p. 38): "O solitary beatitude, o beatific solitude!" (p. 35) With his apophatic metaphors, which un-say his very words, Nasr stresses that his spiritual state cannot be grasped by language. His ecstatic state of Union frees him not only from the constraining experience of time and space, but from his rational, limited mind as well.

The merciful effacement of the *homo viator's* earthly path is again expressed in traditional Sufi symbols. Nasr is opening up the Sufi *trobar clus* to the West, which is no small endeavor. Now he yearns to be once more under the shade of the Blessed Olive Tree of Sura XXIV: 35, which is "neither of the East nor of the West, / whose oil well nigh would shine, even if no fire would touch it". And the poet implores:

O Blessed Olive Tree,
Do thyself again to us unveil,
Wed Heaven and Earth in that unity of early morn.
Return the center to the circle of our earthly life. (p. 46)

The East and the West, Heaven and Earth are merged in otherworldly nuptials in Nasr's inspired verses.

The poet makes repeated use of the geometric figure of the circle, an obvious symbol of infinity for it has no beginning nor end, to make us aware that our pilgrimage is in the end a circular periplus. This lesson is made explicit again when his personal circumambulation of the Ka'bah—again an "outward pilgrimage"—suddenly acquires a higher mystical meaning:

As I circumambulate Thy House, I turn,
Wading back through the stream of time to my original stature,
As Thou didst create me beyond the travail of time.
Where I am? In Thy Eternal presence.
When does this turning take place?
In the now beyond yesterday and morrow.
And so whithersoever I turn I see Thy House and Thy Presence.[23]
(p. 56)

The poet stands "in awe yet intimacy" (p. 56) before God's House, for the veil of the symbolic pilgrimage has been torn asunder and he clearly realizes that he has reached his sacred origins in the Ka'bah of the heart, the real goal of his Pilgrimage. God resides at the center of his being, an infinitely Transcendent Creator (thus the "awe"), yet a Beloved Who is infinitely near (thus the "intimacy"). The mystical path to the One is circular as well as timeless, for, again, it leads to oneself.

"Living in a time beyond time", (p. 51) the poet realizes that what he perceived before as a "lowly world" (p. 29) is redeemed by the overwhelming presence of God. In the mystery of the *Unus/Ambo*, the poet, utterly "transformed" in God, loves Him with His own Love and

[23] The poets alludes to Sura II: 115.

hears the melody of creation and the song of the cherubim, as he joyfully asserts, "with Thine ears". (p. 25) He is now aware of the cadence of Divine Music, sung "in silent invocation by the mountains and the stars". The "Beauty inviolable" of God's Blessed Names is discovered "in the chanting of the birds and the singing of the whales", (p. 32) while the intense darkness of the night bears "an ocean of luminous stars". (p. 51) Nature is clothed in an immortal gown ("the dress of the return to God", p. 42) when the beauty of the One is reflected upon it. The Beloved is present in the whole of this sanctified Creation:

> In the face of a fair maiden and the flight of a flock of birds,
> In the azure of the sky and the roaring sea,
> In the mane of the mighty lion
> and the hues of the lovely sea urchin. (p. 23)

In the shining darkness of Layla's countenance all nature is now contained and rendered eternal.

With his "tasted knowledge", Seyyed Hossein Nasr"s is a veritable *al-'ārif bi'-Llāh*—a true Gnostic who sees Creation through or by God. He is able to see things *in divinis*, as Adam did in Paradise. He is back in Paradise, back in Pre-Eternity, back in the Alpha, even without having reached the Omega of earthly existence in death. Better still, the Alpha and the Omega turn out to be the same, for distance and time have lost their meaning and have been rendered inoffensive. "Multiplicity gone, unity does alone remain". (p. 51) Eternity is reflected into the present now: sages like our poet know well that they always live in the sacred instant of pre-eternity (*al-azal*), in that "early dawn" in which mankind made his eternal covenant with God. It comes as no surprise now to hear him sing that he lives "in a time beyond time, in changelessness". (p. 51)

God is indeed "for all seasons", (p. 41) "a never interrupted Presence", (p. 43) for the mystic poet. He has taken refuge from the domain of becoming in the "bedrock" and "immutable base" (p. 43) of his existence, which he invokes, in a diamantine image, as "The coldness of the eternal realm into which I gaze, albeit for a moment". (p. 42) "Albeit for a moment": but precisely in that supreme moment (ironically beyond time) that the poet lived in the non-spatial locus of his innermost soul, his earthly chains are broken and his earthly pilgrimage itself comes to an unexpected end. The path is volatilized in an "eternal now", (p. 33) in that "eternal instant from which all things are born", as Nasr expresses so accurately in his philosophical yet sapiental work, *Knowledge and the Sacred*.[24]

When the One is the axis of our existence, our earthly journey turns full circle. Our former linear path suddenly changes into a true *tarīqa*, whose "geometry sublime is intricate beyond our ken" (p. 44): the end is the beginning, Earth and the Heavens are wedded, East and West become united, the darkness of the Night is now like a thousand suns, death is no longer menacing. The Omega meets the Alpha, and the path dissolves: it was never there. Nasr's mystical lesson is indeed awesome: the true goal of our path can be reached *in mezzo del camin di nostra vita* because we have never truly left Eternity.

As the Spanish poet José Angel Valente so vividly points out, a true mystic is torn between *la imposibilidad de decir y la imposibilidad de no decir*: between "the impossibility of saying and the impossibility of not saying". Union with God is utterly inexpressible by language, and yet poets of all religious persuasions have sung it in earnest. They sing not only *ex abundantia cordis*, but to build bridges with others friends of the Path. "Whoever has become separated from one who understands his tongue,/ becomes numb were he to have a hundred songs," (p. 79) laments Rumi in Nasr's delicate English rendition. It is true that both poets can claim that "the state of the ripe, none who is raw understands", (p. 75) but their longing reeds sing generously for all lovers of Layla. Seyyed Hossein Nasr, the philosopher, the historian, the scientist, and specially, the sage, has indeed spent a life "lighting the guiding lamp" (p. 51) for humanity. But especially in the inspired pages of *The Pilgrimage of Life and the Wisdom of Rumi*, he succeeds in dispensing the elixir of God's grace from the hallowed chalice of his innermost soul. A lofty *homo viator* and veritable "Inner guide to the One", Nasr leads the Way and urges us to dissolve into Unity "the Alpha and Omega of our life". (p. 54)

LUCE LÓPEZ-BARALT
Universidad de Puerto Rico

[24] *Knowledge and the Sacred* (Crossroads Publishing Co: New York, 1981), p. 228.

Prelude

Seeing with the Eye of the Beloved

When my Beloved appears,
With which eyes do I behold Her?
With Her eyes, not with mine.
For no one does Her but Herself see.

Ibn 'Arabī

(adapted from a poem by Ibn 'Arabi which appears in chapter 63 of his *Futūhat*)

Part I
Journey to the One

The Countenance of the Beloved

هو

صنما من نمی دانم کجایی

گهی ظاهر گهی باطن کجایی

تویی پیدا تویی پنهان در این دار

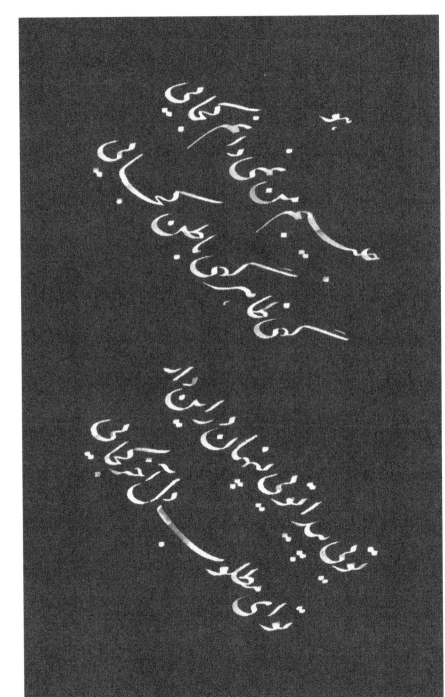

تو ای مطلوب دل آخر کجایی

The Beauty of Layla's Face

O Layla, o beauty of the Night, more luminous than a thousand suns,
Dark because of the abundance of Thy radiance.
We were born to behold the Beauty of Thy Face,
We were born to hear the Beauty of Thy Voice.
Thou art the Essence, darkness shining as the desert sun at noon,
Thy Beauty is in all creatures reflected here below.
In the face of a fair maiden and the flight of a flock of birds,
In the azure sky and the roaring sea,
In the mane of the mighty lion and the hues of the lovely sea urchin.
I hear the Beauty of Thy Voice in the siren song of the whale,
As well in the chant of the nightingale in the garden,
Hymning Thy Praise in her morning concert.
Above all I behold Thy Beauty in the sanctified soul of Thy true lovers,
Beholden to Thy Love, basking in Thy Radiance.

O lovers of Layla, let us remain forever open to beauty,
Let us keep the windows of the soul open to that cool breeze,
Flowing from the horizons beyond to bring us
    the message of our Beloved.
Let us keep our inner ears open to that celestial music,
To the song of the wing of Gabriel which is the root of our very being.
Let us cling to all beauty which a reflection of Her Beauty is.

O Layla, the goal of all my life is to experience Thy Embrace,
To become drowned in the ocean of Thy Beauty in the eternal now,
To become immersed in that Beauty which is also peace,
Peace, calm, harmony, away from all dispersion, from the world's din,
And yet peace which is also ardent love that burns and consumes.
O Layla, Thy Beauty is both light that frees and love that immolates,
The Reality that both illuminates and pacifies,
Bringing a peace that is also supreme ecstasy.
All joys we experience here below and can experience
    from that Beauty come.

O friends of the Path, let us then never forget why we were born.
Into this world we were brought to behold the Beauty of Layla's Face,
To see that Beauty in all that beautiful is,
To hear the Beauty of Her Voice in the hymning of Her Praise,
By all creatures whose very existence is their chant in prayer,
Offered to the Beauty of Layla,
    the Light of whose countenance is the inner reality of all beings.
Let us, o friends, remain true to ourselves, to our true nature,
And behold always the Beauty of Layla's Face, knocking at Her door,
Until we are granted intimacy and are received in Her Embrace.

Bethesda, Maryland
June 25, 2005

I Love Thee with Thy Love

I love Thee with Thy love,
I behold Thy Face with Thine eyes,
I hear the melody of Thy creation,
The chanting of the cherubim with Thine ears.
Thou hast given the Command Be* to all things,
My being a response to that Command appears.
But nay, both Command and response are Thine.
Thou art the Beloved and the lover,
Thou art the seer and the seen.
From Thee flows that celestial music,
And to Thee belongs the ear which that music hears.
Yes, Thou art the source of both the Command and the response.
What then is my reality, my share
In this sublime drama of existence?
My share is none other than poverty,
That mirror which reflects, that emptiness which receives.
What can I offer Thee but this nothingness?
What can I present before Thy resplendent Throne,
But the poverty of Thy devotee and lover?
Accept through Thy Grace this humble offering,
Which yet is the whole being of Thy creature,
Seeking intimacy in that inner chamber,
Where the lover in the embrace of the Beloved melts.

San Juan, Puerto Rico
October 17, 2003

* "God said, 'Be' and there was." (Quran, XXXVI; 82)

I am Near

"I am Near," Thou didst say, assuring Thy servants,
"I answer the call of the caller who calls."*
I call upon Thee now with my being entire,
I call upon Thee in prayer and supplication,
I call upon Thee with invocation and remembrance.
Where is Thy answer? I am all ears to hear Thy response.
I journey in these vast dales and valleys,
Crossing expanses both awesome and full of beauty,
Expanses threatening yet exhilarating.
In traveling towards Thee, I am alone yet not alone,
For Thou didst say Thou art near.
This I know, but let me feel Thy Nearness here and now.
Let me also be near, let me bathe in Thy Nearness.
But as I wonder about Thine answer, I ask,
Is not my call upon Thee itself Thine answer?
For it is Thy Nearness that allows me to call;
Without Thy Nearness how could I upon Thee call?
Let me then remain aware of this holy Nearness,
As I march towards that meeting which is life's goal,
The meeting with Thy Countenance, with Thy Presence.
The meeting between Thou who art and I who am not.
Let me feel Thy Nearness, let me rest in Thine embrace.

Washington
February 23, 2005

---

* In the Noble Quran God states while addressing the Prophet, "When my servants ask thee concerning Me, verily I am near. I answer the call of the caller who calls on Me." (II; 186)

Gnosis and Self-Knowledge

بو

ز عشقت آنچنان مستم که دیگر خود نمی دانم
در این مستی ندانم حیرانم با این حال خاموشم

ز حسن گلستانهای ای ساقی که جامم را طلب باشد
بده یک جرعه زان باده بریزم در دو عالم بو

نه دوران بود و نه مکان تو آغوش ازل باشی
ز روی لطف مشکلات دل را چاره می جویم

در این عالم تو را دارم تو را دارم به تنهایی
وصالت غایت عمرم در این ره پنهان گویم

در این بستر ز دست بی کسی غمی بر جانم
در این بستر ز داروی شراب محبت

به دو شور لطافت هیچ آتش در روان من
در این آتش همی سوزم و دل فانی و خاموش

Let us not Forget

Let us not forget who we are, whence we came, where we shall go;
Let us not forget that pre-eternal day when we bore witness,
Bore witness to His Lordship with a resounding yea,
Which does still echo under the vaults of the celestial realm.

Let us not forget the intimacy of the Beloved's embrace,
The warmth of Her bosom when we in union were.
We have now fallen and forgotten who we are,
Wandering on earth with no compass in hand.

But we can remember, so let us not forget.
Let us not forget that although cast in this lowly world,
Although blinded by veils of neglect and heedlessness,
Although forgetfulness our second nature has become,
We are placed here on earth to remember and can remember.

Let us not forget then to remember our Origin and End,
To remember who we really are as we make this journey of earthly life.

Bethesda, Maryland
The Day before the
Persian New Year,
Norouz of 2005

Human Beings are Asleep—
*When They Die They Awaken**

Did not the Blessed Prophet, he whose heart was always awake,
Utter that we are asleep and awaken when we die?
Who is it who is asleep?
Who is it who awakens?
Here below we dream the dream of negligence,
Imagining ourselves awake, yet slumbering.
The ego asserts itself as the subject that dreams,
Claiming to be awake, yet it is but a sleep-walker.
Let this ego die that voluntary death,
Before the angel of death shatters the pillars of thy earthly existence.
Let the Self awaken within thee,
And know, it is the World Soul that dreameth the ego and the world.
We are but the dream of that One who yet sleeps not.
Awaken now to that Reality which thy dreamy eyes,
Blinking in the darkness cannot perceive.
Awaken while the gift of this miraculous now,
Is still present before thee, the gift of the All-Merciful.
Awaken unto the world of light from that murky existence,
That thy ego mistakes for reality.
Let thy heart awaken to His call,
And see thy ego and the world as a dream,
From which thou has already awakened.
For he who has already awakened here and now has died to the world;
He will not die when the angel of death knocketh at the door.

Conceived in Konya, Turkey
Completed in Bethesda, Maryland
Ramadān 1418
January 1998

* Saying (*hadīth*) of the Prophet.

The Luminous Wine of Gnosis

My blood grows cold, its drops heavy,
Life itself seems dry, the soul a desiccated landscape.
Then miraculously I discover that mysterious Cup,
Thy Cup filled with the Luminous Wine of gnosis.
As I drink this pure Wine, its heat warms my blood,
Its light turns each of its drops into a particle of light,
And the drops now luminous flow, guided to the heart,
Finding their way to the Sun at the Center where Thou resideth,
The Center which was always there, but I knew not.
My body now luminous, I have become a man of light.
My soul no longer the dead earth in which nothing grew,
But a garden where the flowers of Gnosis bloom,
A garden which is a reflection of the Garden of Thy Presence.
O Divine Saki, keep pouring Thy Luminous Wine,
For my thirst ceases not until I become I,
Embraced by Thy Love, immersed in Thy Light.
O Sun of all suns, every luminous drop of my blood,
Every particle of my being flows towards Thee,
O Sun residing at the Center of my heart,
O Source of all Mercy, how can I Thee thank,
For that Luminous Wine of Gnosis, that Wine pure,
Which Thou hast poured into my thirsty soul,
The Wine that has made my blood luminous,
That has turned my being into a ray of light,
To be reabsorbed into the Light that is Thy Light,
Into the Source of my being, the Source of all that is.

Washington, DC
March 6, 2005

The Cadence of Divine Music

On that moment before all moments,
On that morn before the world was born,
When we did Thy Lordship witness,
Seeing Thy Countenance, hearing Thy Command,
Uttering the yea that echoes forever within,
Did we the cadence of Divine Music hear.

In this lowly world I hear that Music near and far,
In the plucking of the ud and the tar,
In the drone of the sitar and the gong of the gamelan,
In the haunting melodies of those monks
Singing in unison of Thy Glory,
In the rhythmic drum beats issuing from verdant forests,
And the shepherd's ney breathing upon the hills,
In all those voices chanting of the love for Thee,
In all music that celebrates Thy Beauty inviolable,
I do hear that cadence of Divine Music,
And so in the chanting of the birds and the singing of the whales,
In the murmur of the wind through those majestic trees,
And even in the silent invocation of the mountains and the stars,
For is not the substance of all Thy creation,
But invocation of Thy Blessed Names
    chanted in the cadence of Divine Music?

But most of all it is in solitude with Thee,
When I and Thou are alone in intimacy,
That I hear so clearly the cadence of that Music Divine
Which I heard on that pre-eternal dawn,
And which ceases not to resonate within,
Bearing witness to the reality of Thy Presence,
Echoing the cadence of that Divine Music,
Echoes from the myriads of created beings
That are but nothingness reflecting Thy Theophanies.

Let me be alone in Thy intimacy,
So as to hear again in the clearest of sounds,
The cadence of that Music Divine
Which I heard at the moment of encounter with Thy Face,
In that pre-eternal moment of creation,
The moment that is now and ever shall be the eternal now.

Paris
May 16, 1999

Alone with the Alone

Thou art the Alone, Thou art the All-One,
To be in solitude is with that One to be.
There was the day when alone by myself,
I was immersed in thoughts, in images and memories drowned,
Alone yet not alone, but with soul like dust scattered,
Dust of manyness veiling the One, veiling the Alone.
Solitude was daydreaming and not beatitude.
But Thou didst shower Thy Grace upon me,
And Thy Light did into my very being enter.
My soul collected, its very substance pierced,
Pierced by Thy Light, by Thy Grace transformed.

My thoughts are now of Thee, my images of Thy Beauty,
My memories dissolved in Thy remembrance.
How to thank Thee that now when alone,
Being alone is being alone with the Alone,
My soul raised above earthly bounds.
For in the courtyard of intimacy of the All-One,
I am naught or all, beyond separation.
Naught and all, extinction and union.
Solitude now no longer endless dreaming,
Immersion in the vortex of endless thoughts,
Being caught in the web of a subjectivity that Thee veils.

Solitude is now beatitude, being alone with the Alone.
And so I sing with Thy friends of old,
O solitary beatitude, o beatific solitude!
Grant me to be always alone, not with myself but with Thee,
Alone with the Alone, the All-One who alone is.
O solitary beatitude, o beatific solitude!

Bethesda, Maryland
June 25, 2004

The Chalice

With Thy Hands didst Thou mold us into a chalice,
On that pre-eternal dawn of our creation,
And Thou didst breathe into us Thy Spirit,
Which a sweet nectar became,
Filling the chalice of our existence.
But here below that dawn now forgotten,
We have become chalices filled with pungent liquid.
The sweet nectar turned into bitter poison,
As remembrance has forgetfulness become.

We cannot the chalice of our existence destroy,
Made as it is by Thy Holy Hands,
But Thou hast given us the gift of emptying the poison.
Let us then pour away this odious water of heedlessness,
And prepare the chalice of our being to be filled,
To receive again the nectar of remembrance.
Let us recall that we were created to be a chalice,
To receive the elixir of Thy Grace and Mercy,
To dispense it to the world at whose center we stand.

Let us again a sacred chalice become,
Before the angel of death brings the curtain down on our life,
And deprives us from becoming here and now,
The chalice filled with the nectar of grace,
As we were at the dawn of creation,
Become a chalice of grace through our will fee,
Before the advent of death removes this freedom,
And breaks the chalice of our earthly existence.

If we become again a hallowed chalice here below,
Thy Spirit we shall bear beyond the gate of death,
But if we leave the world, a chalice desecrated,
Lost as we are to our own inner nature,
Shall we still Thy Spirit bear,
Usurped as is the container Thou didst make?
Woe unto us if a hallowed chalice we not become again,
Before the angel of death breaks the chalice of our earthly life.

La Jolla, California
March 10, 1999

Bewilderment is Victory

O wonder of creation wonder bewildered at the wonder of creation,
Cast aside conjecture, mental play,
Break the prison of all that binds,
Wonder in awe with all thy being at the mystery of Being,
At the starry heavens and the luminous dawn,
At all that is, all that becomes, at the mystery of nothingness,
At forms so diverse, born to die and yet be reborn.
Break the prison of all that binds,
And be free in bewilderment,
Whence we come and whither we go,
Wonder at the two great unknowns binding the book of thy life.
Then lo, break this binding and swim in that Infinite Ocean,
Swim bewildered in that Boundless Ocean Divine.
Bewilderment is indeed victory,
Victory over all accidents of earthly life,
Wonder bewildered for it is in bewilderment
    that the final victory cometh.

Bethesda
March 20, 2000
Norouz of 1379 (A.H. solar)

This poem was inspired by the verse of Jalāl al-Dīn Rumī:

> *Sell cleverness and buy bewilderment.*
> *For cleverness is conjecture and bewilderment victory.*

The Theophanic Presence of the Beloved in Creation

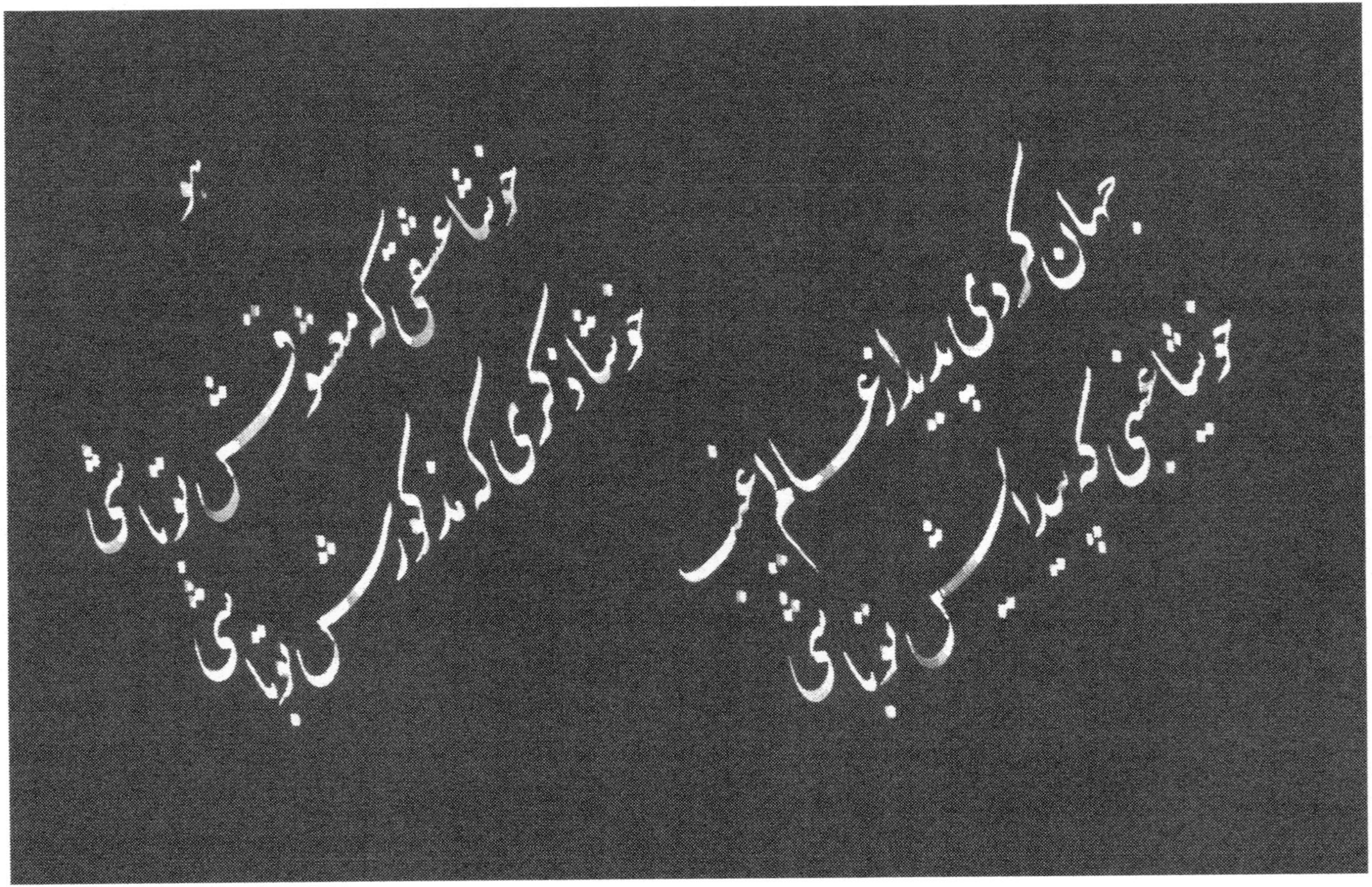
هو
خوشا عشقی که معشوقش تو باشی
خوشا ذکری که مذکورش تو باشی
جهان کردی پدید از عالم عشق
خوشا عینی که پیدایش تو باشی

Thou art for All Seasons

My life has many a season seen,
Spring into Summer turns, Autumn Winter becomes.
Yet Thou remaineth, Thou art for all seasons.
Blossoms and fresh leaves adorn the trees,
Leaves dressed in light green, yet to see the solar light.
Meadows turn into emerald carpets, flowers bloom.
The soul takes joy in this spring rebirth,
But the blossoms fall and the cool breeze warm becomes,
How sad that this splendor lasts but a fleeting moment.
Yet Thou remaineth, Thou art for all seasons.

To Summer I turn accustomed to its long days,
To the vivid green of the valley and dale,
The soul becomes anchored in this Summer rhythm,
And yet hardly has the anchor sunk into the Summer sea,
When the ship of the soul has to set sail again,
As Summer into Autumn turns, leaving in its trail,
Nostalgia for a period of gentler rhythms gone by.
Yet Thou remaineth, Thou art for all seasons.

How refreshing the Autumn wind, it cools body and soul,
How wondrous the symphony of colors,
The dress of the Return to God worn by His creation,
At the moment of a death that is prelude to life anew.
But before my eyes are satiated by all this beauty,
The leaves fall, the birds to far away horizons fly,
Where are all the harmony and joy of those colored trees,
Gently moving with the Autumnal wind,
In invocation of His Blessed Name.
Yes, how fleeting all this joy, how transient this Fall beauty.
Yet Thou remaineth, Thou art for all seasons.

At last the cold and snowy Winter,
Nature is asleep and the wintry air has come,
Invigorating body and soul and turning life within.
Still, how calming the fall of those snowflakes,
How humbling the rigor of these Winter storms.
To this season I have become accustomed,
Sitting by the warmth of fire to behold the icy world without.
But again hand and feet have hardly warm become,
When the ice melts, into rain does the snow turn,
New gentler winds blow, heralding Spring's coming.
How passing the joys of this season of crystalline images,
Of the cold which also to the celestial realm belongs,
A coldness beyond the heat that corrupts earthly life,
The coldness of the eternal realm into which I gaze,
    albeit for but a moment.
Yet Thou remaineth, Thou art for all seasons.

As the seasons pass, so does my life.
Where is the stable foundation, where the firm bedrock?
The seasons return, but my life moves on,
Like an arrow shot from the Master's bow,
Racing to the target inevitable which is death, meeting with Thee.
But in this earthly life through which the seasons flow,
Where do I find that permanence for which I yearn?
Where do I stand to observe the seasons' march,
A march from year to year until life's own season ends?
The answer resides in Thy never interrupted Presence.
Thou art here and now in the balmy Spring and hot Summer,
Thou art here and now in the windy Fall and blustery Winter.
What care I if the seasons pass, Thou art near.
Time flows by and seasons change.
Yet Thou remaineth, Thou art for all seasons.
The bedrock of my existence, its immutable base,
The Alpha from which I hail, the Omega to which I return.

20 Ramaḍān 1483 A.H.
(the night of the martyrdom of 'Alī)
November 25, 2002

*Autumn is the Spring of the Gnostics**

From the moment we into this world are born,
Our journey begins to the Origin from which we came.
Our life is a readying for that Return,
Return to whence it all began.
Nature's ever recurrent rhythms this truth reveal,
And remind us through the birth and death,
Spring and Autumn of vegetal life,
Of that great cycle of our own earthly existence,
Whose Omega is the Return to the Alpha, the All.

With the Autumn breeze the tree colors turn,
Forests become a rainbow of shimmering hues,
Yellows and purples and reds vie with the greens,
In a geometry sublime, intricate beyond our ken,
To create a symphony of forms of endless beauty.
Nature dresses in her most noble garb,
To be worthy of being present before that Majestic King,
To whom all things do return.
And return it does as its colors diminish,
As hues fade away into a subtle colorlessness,
Which yet all colors contains, a death which is also new life.

---

* This is a famous Sufi saying (*khazân bahâr-i 'urafâst*).

The gnostic lives in this world of change,
Aware constantly of the Return,
The Return which the origin of true life is.
He sees in Autumn's majesty, that Return for which he yearns,
Which for him is the Spring of heavenly life.
If Spring be the origin of life below,
Autumn is the Spring of eternal life,
That life for the Return to which the gnostic lives here on earth.
And so for him Autumn is the Spring of life divine,
Heralding the Return to that life that never ends.

Written in the autumn of 2001
Bethesda, Maryland

*O Blessed Olive Tree**

O Blessed Olive Tree,
Neither of East nor West art thou,
Yet, thy Light doth all the lamps illumine,
That in East and West for His Glory shine.

Thou art the axis of our world,
The pole that unites Heaven and Earth,
And center too of our circle of existence.
Why then hast thou from us absent become?

Now, Earth is rent from its heavenly consort,
And we are left lost in a circle that centerless is.
O Blessed Olive Tree,
Do thyself again to us unveil,
Wed Heaven and Earth in that unity of early morn.
Return the center to the circle of our earthly life.

In need of thee we are as never before,
In a world of chaos for centerless it is,
Of darkness for it lacks the light of the lamp,
Illuminated through the burning of the oil,
Of that olive which thou bringeth forth.

O Blessed Olive Tree,
Thy reality to us do manifest,
When we are in the direst need,
Of thy presence as the axis of our world,
As the center of our circle of existence,
Of thy Light as the sacred reality
In which East and West can again united become,
As they were in creation's dawn,
When thy Light upon us all did shine.

Bethesda, Maryland
August 17, 2002

---

* The Blessed Olive Tree is in reference to the "Light" verse of the Quran (24; 35):

Allah is the Light of the heavens and the earth. The similitude of His light is as a niche wherein is a lamp. The lamp is in a glass. The glass is as it were a shining star. (This lamp is) kindled from a blessed tree, an olive neither of the East nor of the West, whose oil would almost glow forth (of itself) though no fire touched it. Allah guideth unto His Light whom He will. And Allah speaketh to mankind in symbols, for Allah is Knower of all things.

Pilgrimage to Holy Sites

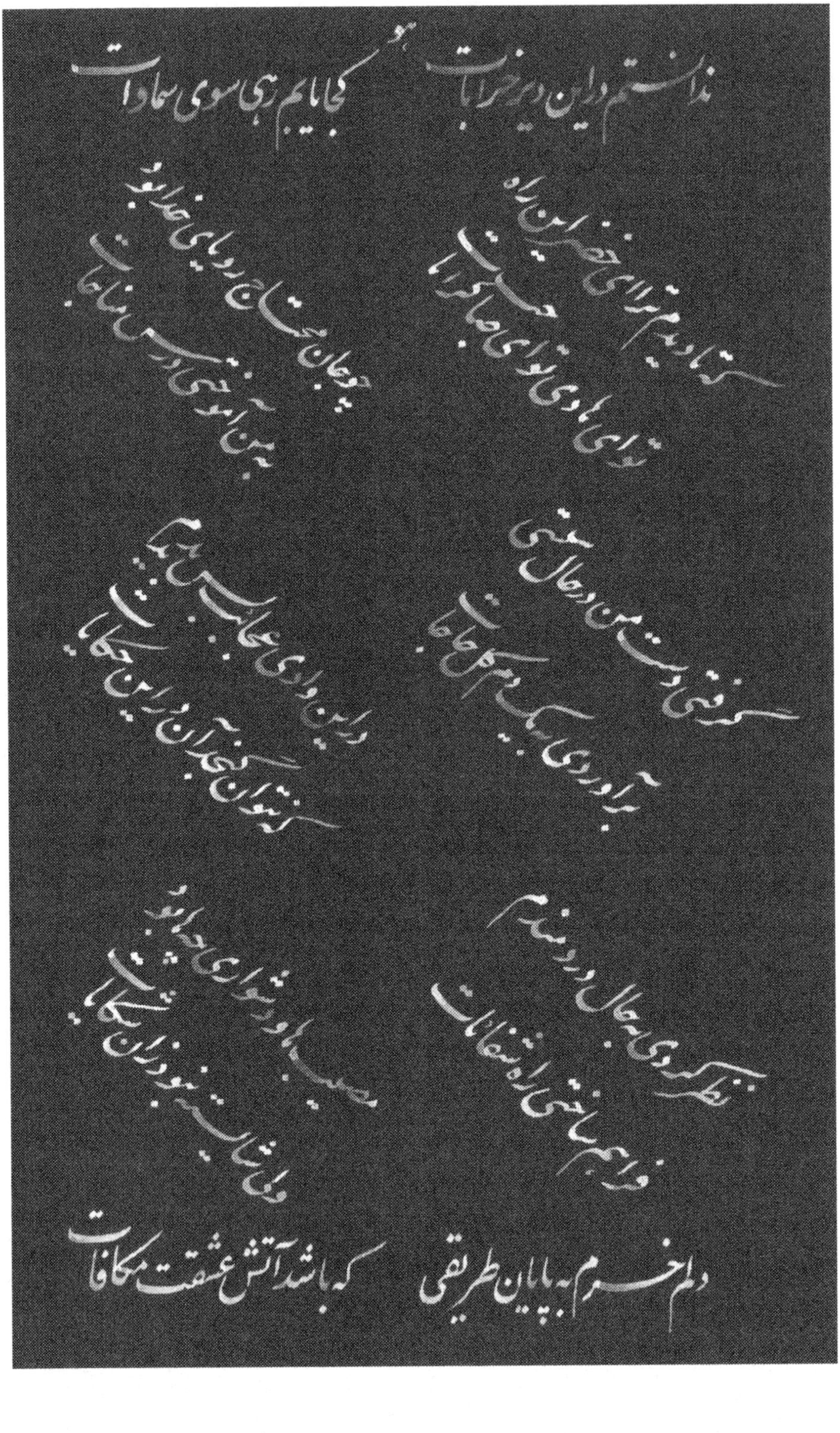
هو
ندانستم درین دیر خرابات
کجا یابم رهی سوی سعادات
دلم خرم به پایان طریقت
که باشد آتش عشقت مکافات

Humaythara[*]

Humaythara, hidden sanctuary, blessed center,
Veiled from eyes that from the Truth are veiled.
Humaythara, hidden far away in the desert pure,
Guarded by hills and mountains stark,
Crowned by the majesty of the crystal realm.
Dunes stretching into the endless horizons,
Vast spaces where Bedouins alone breathe,
Those for whom yesterday tomorrow is, and tomorrow today,
Living in a time beyond time, in changelessness,
Always aware of the sacred precinct in their midst,
Humaythara of which they the guardians are.
The light of the sun in day all forms dissolves,
Multiplicity gone, unity does alone remain.
At night the awe of the dark sky the soul does overcome,
Darkness so intense yet bearing an ocean of luminous stars.
The night sky so full of celestial lights,
As if their very multitude would the heavenly dome break,
And the starlight would engulf as here below.

---

* The burial site of Shaykh Abu'l-Hasan al-Shādhilī in the southern Egyptian desert.

Humaythara, thou containeth in thy holy soil,
The earthly remains of the Pole of those who know,
Abu'l-Hasan who in this blessed place did die,
Far from the slopes of those verdant mountains where he was born.
Between the Maghrib and this ancient Egypt,
A life spent in lighting the guiding lamp,

Whose rays shine forth to this day from the China Sea,
To where the Atlantic washes Muslim shores,
And even beyond to the abode of the setting sun.
And so men and women from near and distant lands,
To thy welcoming bosom come to be by thy grace blessed,
By that noble presence in thy midst preserved.

O Humaythara do thy treasure well guard,
The treasure that God hath to Thee bestowed,
To protect, to cherish, in safety to keep.
O hidden center of a grace whose perfume,
Is by the winds to the four corners scattered,
May God guard thee from the din of the world,
And thy silence protect for those who that silence seek,
The silence that is presence of that remembrance,
For whose sake Abu'l-Hasan was to our circle sent,
By Him Whose remembrance is life's supreme goal.

Cairo
September 15, 2001
Shortly after a pilgrimage to
Humaythara

Marrakesh

Verdant oasis rising amidst the sand,
Tied to Heaven by exalted peaks,
Rooted in this sandy earth with reddish hue,
Reflecting the expanses of the horizon when,
After her daily journey the sun does set,
Oasis at the heart of this land of evening light.

Saints and heroes fill the space of life,
They do remain, reminders of a glorious past,
And source of the ever present *barakah* that all permeates.
Seven among the friends of God this city do guard,
And are its gates to the heavenly realm.
Seven sanctuaries with spiritual presence filled,
Like the seven energy centers of the temple that the body is.
Seven like the seven days of a week of life,
Seven like the seven planets wandering above,
Seven friends of God in whose number time and space,
These matrices of our earthly life united are.

In their sanctuaries I hear voices chanting of love and knowledge,
Of the One who alone is, is now and ever shall be,
All space near and far contracted to the Center that here is.

How blessed to breathe the sacred air of this oasis,
To bathe in the grace inundating us from the remains,
The earthly remains of those who having reach the Goal,
And are forever with us here, now, in proximity to Him and us,
Inner guides to the One, the Alpha and Omega of our life.

Marrakesh
September 13, 2004

Circumambulating the Ka'bah

Here stands the House of God, majestic yet intimate,
Symbol of the Transcendent who yet near is,
Emptiness and fullness, presence and truth.
The primordial temple dressed in black vestment,
Mystery of mysteries, adorned by the golden letters,
Of the last Word revealed to the Last of Prophets
By the One, by the God of Adam and Abraham,
Prophets who this most ancient of sacred abodes did build.

Countless men and women circumambulate this hub,
Center of the world of those in surrender to the Master of the House,
From every clime, of every color, with diverse speech,
Yet with a single voice—"at Thy service," "at Thy service,"
Rotating in harmony around the Ka'bah,
Image of the heavens turning around the polar star,
And of the angels in adoration around the Divine Throne.
There are many faces, many wills, many hearts,
Yet all reflecting Thy Face, all obeying Thy Will,
With hearts united in beholding that other heart which the Ka'bah is.
The many immersed in Thy Oneness;
    Thy Oneness reflected in the multitudes.

As I circumambulate Thy House, I turn,
Wading back through the stream of time to my original stature,
As Thou didst create me beyond the travail of time.
Where am I? In Thy Eternal Presence.
When does this turning take place?
    In the now beyond yesterday and morrow.
And so whithersoever I turn I see Thy House and Thy Presence.
And whenever I close my eyes to the fleeting images of the world,
I am standing in awe yet intimacy before Thy House,
Before the Ka'bah which also resides at the center of my being.

Conceived in Mecca
Dhu'l-Hijjah 1425
January 2005

The Pilgrimage

All life a pilgrimage is to the threshold of Thy Sacred Presence,
And within that universal pilgrimage, men and women,
Thy creatures from lands near and far, make other pilgrimages,
Holy journeys to this or that site that reflects that Sacred Presence.

But there is a pilgrimage on earth that is *the* Pilgrimage,
The Pilgrimage to that primordial mother of cities, Mecca,
To the Ka'bah which is Thy House here on earth,
Sacred center and earthly locus of the world axis,
For those who follow the last of Thy messages.

The rites are primordial, following in the footsteps,
Imitating the actions of Abraham, Thy Friend,
The Father of that family which to Thy Oneness testify.
Within that climate of Semitic spirituality Thou didst choose
To reveal the ultimate glory of Thy Oneness.

The rites are arduous, the tasks in themselves hard.
Yet, with faith in Thee hardship turns into ease.
Spiritual intensity and physical strain go hand in hand.
The body is pushed to its limits, while the spirit, strengthened,
Declares its victory over all hardships the body endures.

How blessed to accomplish that which Thou hast required of us,
To complete *the* Pilgrimage that is the mother of all pilgrimages,
To realize that even in this world of negligence and forgetfulness,
This ancient rite instituted by Abraham and then revived,
Brought back to life by the last of Thy messengers,
Continues to be performed now as in the days of old,
Bearing testimony to Thy never-ending Lordship,
Bearing witness to the reality of Thy Power and Presence,
Which draw Thy servants, young and old, from East and West,
To the House that is Thy House,
To the city that is Thy city,
To the Pilgrimage that marks supreme surrender to Thy Will.

Conceived in Mecca
Dhu'l-Hijjah 1425
January 2005

سودای عشقت در سرم

سوی ...ت نشینم

دوری ز تو پایان آر

شوق وصالت حاصلم

Thou Hast Departed

How sad to hear that thou hast departed,
Leaving this lowly world for the luminous beyond.
Thy gentle voice, uttering words of wisdom slowly,
Deliberately like honey being gently poured,
Not to be heard again in this transient realm,
Nor thy writings new to be beheld by eager eyes,
Accustomed to the outpouring of pearls of wisdom,
From thy gracious pen for decades on end.

How in days of old we circumambulated the Ka'bah,
And wandered amidst the turquoise blue mosques of Isfahan.
How we paid homage to the saints of Marrakesh,
Walking in remembrance to those sacred sites away hidden.
How oft we visited holy places in Cairo and celebrated His Glory,
On continents stretching from East to West.
These joyous moments are to be no more here below,
How sad then to hear that thou hast departed.

And yet joyous it is indeed to recall thy long life,
A life so rich, bearing so much spiritual fruit,
That has nourished souls from near and far.
Thou hast departed but thy words and memories remain,
Etched on the tablet of our hearts, on the substance of our souls.

Dear friend of God, may the doors of His Grace upon thee open.
May we again by the Kawthar* meet, if He wills,
There to contemplate in harmony the infinite Beauty,
The dazzling Splendor of the Face of the Friend.

Key Biscayne, Florida
May 13, 2005

Written a day after the death of Shaykh Abū Bakr Sirāj al-Dīn al-Shādhilī, al-Darqāwi, al-'Alawī, al-Maryamī—*raḍī Allāhu 'anhu*—to whom this poem is dedicated.

* A river of paradise according to the Quran.

Part II

A Few Moments with Rumi

ای خداوند سخن سلطان عشق — ای که بودی پاسدار راز عشق

هشت قرنی از حیات تو گذشت — ماند باقی در جهان غوغای عشق

مثنویت هست بحر معرفت — معرفت آمیخته با عطر عشق

بود دیوانت پر از شور و طرب — ما از آن حیران در وادی عشق

دانش تو شعر تو احسان تو — هست ما را خضر ره در راه عشق

تو بدی مانوس با آن شمس دین — آتش دیدارتان درگاه عشق

نام تو در این جهان جاوید باد — هست نقش نام تو بر لوح عشق

ای سخنور جملگانت همچو در — برفشاند سر اصطرلاب عشق

میکشانی نفس ما سوی فنا — ما همه در حیرت و فانی عشق

The Commotion of Love

O Master of speech, the King of Love,
O thou who wert the guardian of the secrets of Love.
Eight centuries have passed since thy earthly life,
There has remained in the world the commotion of Love.
Thy *Mathnawī* is the ocean of gnosis,
Gnosis mixed with the perfume of Love.
Thy *Dīwān* is full of ecstasy and joy,
We in wonder before it in the valley of Love.
Thy knowledge, thy poetry, thy virtuous beauty,
Are our Khezr of the path on the road of Love,
Thou wert intimate with that Sun of Religion,
The fire of your meeting the threshold of Love.
May thy name remain forever in this world,
For thy name is inscribed upon the tablet of Love.
O literary master, thy words are like pearls,
Diffusing the secret of the astrolabe of Love.
Thou pullest our souls towards extinction,
We are all in wonder annihilated in Love.

Bethesda, Maryland
January 2007

Dedicated to Jalal al-din Rumi on the occasion of the celebration of his eight hundredth anniversary in Qonya in the Spring of 2007.

چه تدبیرای مسلمانان که من خودرا نمیدانم
نه ترسا نه یهودم من نه گبرم نه مسلمانم

نه شرقیم نه غربیم نه بریم نه بحریم
نه از کان طبیعیم نه از افلاک گردانم

نه از خاکم نه از آبم نه از بادم نه از آتش
نه ازعرشم نه از فرشم نه از کونم نه از کانم

نه از هندم نه از چینم نه از بلغار و سقسینم
نه از ملک عراقینم نه از خاک خراسانم

نه از دنیی نه از عقبی نه از جنت نه از دوزخ
نه از آدم نه از حوا نه از فردوس و رضوانم

مکانم لا مکان باشد نشانم بی نشان باشد
نه تن باشد نه جان باشد که من از جان جانانم

*A ghazal from the Great Dīwān**

What is to be done, O Muslims, for I know myself not,
Neither a Christian am I, nor Jew, no Magean nor Muslim.
Neither of the East am I nor West, nor of the land, nor sea;
Nor of nature's quarry, nor of heavens circling above.
I am not made of earth or water, not of wind or fire;
Nor am I of the Divine Throne nor of floor carpeting,
nor of the domain of the cosmos, nor of minerals.
I am not from India, nor China, nor Bulgaria, nor Turkistan;
I am not from the kingdom of the two Iraqs,
    nor from the earth of Khorasan.
Neither of this world I am nor the next; nor of heaven nor hell;
Nor from Adam nor Eve nor of Eden,
    nor Paradise nor the Supreme Garden.
My place is the placeless, my mark the markless;
Not either body or soul for I Myself the Beloved am.

*Attributed to Rumi

دوئی از خود بدر کردم یکی دیدم دو عالمرا
یکی جویم یکی دانم یکی بینم یکی خوانم

هو الاول هو الاخر هو الظاهر هو الباطن
بجز یا هو و یا من هو کسی دیگر نمی‌دانم

ز جام عشق سرمستم دو عالم رفته از دستم
بجز رندی و قلاشی نباشد هیچ سامانم

اگر در عمر خود روزی دمی بی تو برآوردم
از آن وقت و از آن ساعت زعمر خود پشیمانم

اگر دستم دهد روزی دمی با تو درین خلوت
دو عالم زیر پای آرم همی دستی بر افشانم

الا ای شمس تبریزی چنین مستم درین عالم
که جز مستی و قلاشی نباشد هیچ دستانم

I cast aside duality seeing the two worlds as one,
I seek the One, I know the One, I see the One, I call the One,
He is the First, He is the Last, He is the Outward, He the Inward.*
I know no one other than He, none but He who is He.
Drunk with the goblet of Love I am,
    the two worlds have to me been lost,
No rest I have but in debauchery, no rest but in drunkenness.
If I spent a moment of my life without Thee,
I regret that moment, I for that hour of my life do repent.
If one day I am given a moment with Thee in this retreat,
I shall trample the two worlds underfoot and dance in ecstasy.
O Shams of Tabriz, I am so drunk in this world,
That but for drunkenness and revelry, no story have I to account.**

*This is a Quranic verse cited directly by Rūmī.

** A *ghazal* from the *Dīwān of Rūmī, Selected Poems from Divan-e Shams-e Tabrīzī*, trans. and introduced by R. A. Nicholson (Bethesda, MD: Ibex Publishers, 2001).

Translations from the Mathnawi

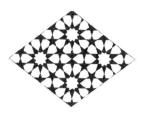

بشنو از نی چون حکایت می کند   از جداییها شکایت می کند

کز نیستان تا مرا ببریده اند   از نفیرم مرد وزن نالیده‌اند

سینه خواهم شرحه شرحه از فراق   تا بگویم شرح درد اشتیاق

هر کسی کو دورماند از اصل خویش   باز جوید روزگار وصل خویش

من به هر جمعیتی نالان شدم   جفت بد حالان و خوش حالان شدم

هر کسی از ظن خود شد یارمن   از درون من نجست اسرار من

سر من از نالهٔ من دور نیست   لیک چشم و گوش را آن نور نیست

تن زجان و جان زتن مستور نیست   لیک کس را دید جان دستور نیست

آتشست این بانگ نای و نیست باد   هر که این آتش ندارد نیست باد

The Exordium of the Mathnawī of Rūmī

In the Name of God—The Infinitely Good, the All-Merciful

I

Listen to the reed, how it narrates a tale,
A tale of all the separations of which it complains.
Ever since they have cut me from the reed-bed,
Men and women have moaned about my lament.
How I wish in separation, a bosom shred and shred,
So as to utter the description of longing's pain.
Whoever becomes distanced from his roots,
Seeks to return to the days of his union.
I joined every gathering uttering my lament,
Consorting with the joyous and the sorrowful.
Everyone befriended me through what he had opined,
But none did seek the secrets within me hidden.
My secret is not far away from my lament,
Yet, the eye and ear do not possess that light.
Body is not hidden from soul, nor soul from body,
Yet, none has the license to see the soul.
The cry of the reed is fire, not wind,
Whoso does not possess this fire may he be naught.

آتـــش عشـــقست کـــانـــدرنـــی فـتـــاد		جـوشـــش عـشقـســـت کـــاندر مـــی‌فتـــاد

نی حـریـــف هـر کـه از یـــاری بـریـــد		پــــرده‌هـــاش پـــــرده‌هـــای مـــا دریـــد

هـمچو نی زهـری وتـریاقـی کـه دیـد؟		همچو نــی دمـساز و مشتاقی کـه دیـــد؟

نی حـدیـث راه پـــر خـــون مـــی کنـد		قـــصه‌هـــای عشــق مـــجنون مـــی کـــند

محـرم ایـن هـوش،جز بیهـوش نیـــست		مـر زبـــان را مشتری ، جز گـوش نیـست

در غـــم مـــا روزهـــا بـــیگاه شـــد		روزهـــا بـــا ســـوزها هـــمراه شـــــد

روزهـا گـر رفـت، گـو رو بـاک نیسـت		تو بمان ای آنکه چـون تـو پـاک نـــیست

هـــر کـــه جـز مـاهی، ز آبش سیر شد		هـر که بـی روزیـــست، روزش دیـر شـد

در نـیابـــد حـــال پختـــه هـــیچ خـــام		پـــس ســـخن کــــوتاه بـــاید،و الـــسلام

'Tis the fire of Love that befelled the reed,
'Tis the ardor of Love that entered the wine.
The reed is the comrade of whoever is severed from a friend,
Its strains have rent asunder our veils.
Who has ever seen a poison and an antidote like the reed?
Who has ever seen a consort and a longing lover like the reed?
The confidante of this sense is none other than the senseless,
For the tongue has no client save the ear.
In our sorrow the days of our life have become untimely,
The days have become fellow travelers of burning grief.
If the days have passed, say go, it matters not,
Do Thou remain, O Thou like whom there is no one pure.
Whoever is other than fish with His water sated becomes,
Whoever has no daily bread, his day stretched becomes,
The state of the ripe, none who is raw understands,
Hence brief my words must be. Farewell.

بند بگسل ، باش آزاد ، ای پسر　　چند باشی بند سیم و بند زر

گر بریزی بحر را در کوزه ای　　چند گنجد؟ قسمت یک روزه ای

کوزه ی چشم حریصان پر نشد　　تا صدف قانع نشد، پر در نشد

هر کرا جامه ز عشقی چاک شد　　او ز حرص و جمله عیبی پاک شد

شاد باش ای عشق خوش سوادی ما　　ای طبیب جمله علتهای ما

ای دوای نخوت و ناموس ما　　ای تو افلاطون و جالینوس ما

جسم خاک از عشق بر افلاک شد　　کوه در رقص آمد و چالاک شد

عشق ، جان طور آمد عاشقا　　طورمست و خر موسی صاعقا

O son, break the chains that bind thee and be free,
For how long wilt thou continue to be a slave of silver and gold.
If thou pourest the sea into a pitcher,
How much will it hold? The share of one day.
The pitcher that is the eye of the covetous never full becomes,
Until the oyster shell is contented, full of pearls it becomes not.
He whose garment is rent by Love,
He alone becomes purified of covetousness and every defect.
Hail to thee o our Love with goodly passion,
O physician of all our ailments,
O remedy of our pride and honor,
O Thou our Plato and Galen besides.
The body of dust has risen to the heavens through Love,
The mountain has begun to dance and become nimble.
O lover, Love became the soul of Mt. Sinai,
Mt. Sinai became drunk and Moses fell into a swoon.

با لب دمساز خود گر جفتمی	همچو نی من گفتنیها گفتمی
هر که او از هم زبانی شد جدا	بی زبان شد گر چه دارد صد نوا
چونک گل رفت و گلستان در گذشت	نشنوی ز آن پس ز بلبل سر گذشت
جمله معشوقست و عاشق پرده ای	زنده معشوقست و عاشق مرده ای
چون نباشد عشق را پروای او	او چو مرغی ماند بی پر، وای او
من چگونه هوش دارم پیش و پس؟	چون نباشد نور یارم پیش و پس
عشق خواهد کین سخن بیرون بود	آینه غماز نبود چون بود؟
آینه ات دانی چرا غماز نیست؟	ز آنکه زنگار از رخش ممتاز نیست

If my lips were to be joined with a kindred soul,
Like the reed I would tell that which could be told.
Whoever has become separated from one who understands his tongue,
Becomes dumb were he to have a hundred songs.
When the flower departs and the rose garden fades,
Thou hearest no longer the story of the nightingale.
The Beloved is all, the lover but a veil,
The Beloved is alive, the lover but a dead being.
When Love no longer cares for him,
He becomes like a bird without feather, alas for him!
How can I have consciousness before and after,
If the light of my Friend not be before and after?
Love wills that this word be cast forth,
If the mirror does not reflect, how is that so?
Doest thou know why thy mirror nothing reflects?
Because the rust has not become cleansed from its face.

Book I – v. 1-35

دید از زاریش، کو زار دلست		تن خوشست و او گرفتار دلست

عاشقی پیداست از زاری دل		نیست بیماری، چو بیماری دل

علت عاشق ز علتها جداست		عشق، اصطرلاب اسرار خداست

عاشقی گر زین سر و گر ز آن سرست		عاقبت ما را بدان سر رهبرست

هرچ گویم عشق را شرح و بیان		چون بعشق آیم خجل باشم از آن

گرچه تفسیر زبان روشن گرست		لیک، عشق بی زبان روشن ترست

چون قلم اندر نوشتن می‌شتافت		چون بعشق آمد قلم برخود شکافت

عقل در شرحش چو خر در گل بخفت		شرح عشق و عاشقی هم عشق گفت

II

He saw from her grief that it was the grief of the heart,
The body was well, but she was heart stricken.
Being in love is manifested by grief of the heart,
There is no sickness like sickness of the heart.
The disease of the lover is other than all other diseases,
Love is the astrolabe of God's mysteries.
Whether being in love be from the side here below or the side yonder,
In the end it is our guide to the side beyond.
Whatever description or explanation I give of Love,
When I reach Love I am ashamed of my exposition.
Although commentary by the tongue clarifies,
Love that is tongueless is of greater clarity.
As the pen was hastening to write,
When it came to Love it split upon itself.
In expounding Love, reason becomes mired like an ass in mud,
It was Love alone that Love and being in love has explained.

Book I – v. 108-115

ز آنک عشق مردگان پاینده نیست   ز آنک مرده سوی ما آینده نیست

عشق زنده، در روان و در بصر   هر دمی باشد زغنچه تازه تر

عشق آن زنده گزین، کو باقیست   کز شراب جان فزایت ساقیست

عشق آن بگزین که جمله انبیا   یافتند از عشق او کار و کیا

تو مگو : ما را بدان شه بار نیست   با کریمان، کارها دشوار نیست

III

For the love of the dead endures not,
For the dead one never to us returns.
But the Love of the living, in our spirit and vision,
Is fresher at every moment than a bud.
Choose the Love of that Living One who is everlasting,
Who poureth the wine which increases thy spirit.
Choose Love of that One through whose Love,
All the prophets success achieved and glory gained.
Say not, "For us there is no way of access to that King,"
With help of the generous, actions are not difficult.

Book I, v. 218-222

سیر بیرون نیست قول و فعل ما   سیر باطن هست بالای سما

حس خشکی دید کز خشکی بزاد   عیسی جان، پای بر دریا نهاد

سیر جسم خشک ، برخشکی فتاد   سیرجان پا در دل دریا نهاد

چونک عمر اندر ره خشکی گذشت   گاه کوه و گاه دریا، گاه دشت

آب حیوان از کجا خواهی تو یافت؟   موج دریا را کجا خواهی شکافت؟

موج خاکی وهم و فهم و فکر ماست   موج آبی محو و سکرست و فناست

تا درین سکری، از آن سکری تو دور   تا ازین مستی، از آن جامی تو کور

گفت و گوی ظاهر آمد چون غبار   مدتی خاموش خو کن، هوش دار!

IV

Our words and actions are the outward journey,
The inner journey above the heavens resides.
The sense saw dry land, as it was of dryness born,
But the Jesus of the spirit, set foot upon the Sea.
The journey of the body of dryness fell on dry earth,
The journey of the spirit set foot in the heart of the Sea.
Since thy life has passed on dry land,
Now mountain, now river, now desert,
Whence wilt thou the Water of Life find?
Where wilt thou cleave the waves of the Sea?
The earthly waves are our fantasy, understanding and thought,
The Sea waves are self-effacement, drunkenness and annihilation.
While thou art in this worldly drunkenness,
 thou art from that drunkenness far removed,
While thou art drunken with this, thou art blind to that cup.
Outward discourse is like dust,
Learn the habit of silence for awhile, take heed!

Book I, v. 574-586

ماعـــــدمهاییم و هســـــتیهای مـــا   تـــو وجـــود مطلقـــی فـــانی نمـــا

مـــا همـــه شـــیران، ولـــی شـــیرعلم   حملـــه شـــان از بـــاد باشـــد دم بـــه دم

حملـــه شـــان پیـــدا و ناپیداســـت بـــاد   آنکـــه ناپیداســـت از مـــا گـــم مبـــاد!

بـــاد مـــا و بـــود مـــا از داد توســـت   هســـتی مـــا جملـــه از ایجـــاد توســـت

لـــذت هســـتی نمـــودی نیســـت را   عاشـــق خـــود کـــرده بـــودی نیســـت را

لـــذت انعـــام خـــود را وا مگیـــر   نقـــل و بـــاده ، جـــام خـــود را وا مگیـــر

ور بگیـــری، کیســـت جســـت و جـــو کنـــد؟   نقـــش بـــا نقـــاش چـــون نیـــرو کنـــد؟

منگـــر انـــدر مـــا، مکـــن در مـــا نظـــر   انـــدر اکـــرام و ســـخای خـــود نگـــر

مـــا نبـــودیم و تقاضـــامان نبـــود   لطـــف تـــو ناگفتـــه ی مـــا مـــی‌شـــنود

V

We are nonexistent and so is our existence,
Thou art Absolute Being, appearing in the guise of the perishable.
We are all lions, but lions on a flag,
Whose charge from the wind moment to moment comes.
Their charge is manifest but the wind hidden,
May that which is hidden be not lost to us!
Our wind and our existence issue from Thy gift,
Our whole existence by Thee bestowed.
Thou didst show the joy of existence to the non-existent,
Thou didst make the non-existent Thy lover.
Do not take away the joy of Thy bounty,
Do not take away the sweet, the wine and the cup.
Wert Thou to take them away, who would be there to inquire?
How could a painting test strength with the painter?
Look at us not, fix Thy gaze upon us not,
Look on Thine own honor and generosity.
We were not and we had no demands,
Thy grace was hearkening to our silent words.

Book I, v. 606-614

گر تـو صـد سیب و صـد آبـی بشـمری		صـد نمانـد، یـک شـود چـون بفشـری

در معـانی، قسـمت و اعـداد نیسـت		در معـانی تجزیـه و افـراد نیسـت

اتحـاد یـار بـا یـاران خـوش اسـت		پای معنـی گیـر، صـورت سـرکش اسـت

صـورت سـرکش گـدازان کـن بـرنج		تـا ببینـی زیـر او وحـدت چـو گـنج

ور تـو نگـدازی عنایتهـای او		خـود گـدازد ای دلـم مـولای او

او نمایـد هـم بـدلها خـویش را		او بـدوزد خرقـه درویـش را

VI

Wert thou to count a hundred apples, a hundred quinces,
The hundred would remain not but become one,
    when together they are pressed.
In matters spiritual there is no partition, no numbers,
In matters spiritual there is no division, no individuals.
The union of the Friend with friends is sweet,
Grab the foot of spiritual reality, for the outward form does rebel.
Through tribulation cause the rebellious form to dissolve,
So that thou mayest see beneath it unity like a treasure.
If thou dost dissolve it not, His favors,
They will it dissolve—o my heart which His vassal is.
He even revealeth to the hearts His Self,
He seweth the patched frock of the dervish.

منبسط بودیم و یک جوهر همه   بی سر و بی پا بدیم آن سر همه

یک گهر بودیم همچون آفتاب   بی گره بودیم و صافی همچو آب

چون بصورت آمد آن نور سره   شد عدد چون سایه‌های کنگره

کنگره ویران کنید از منجنیق   تا رود فرق از میان این فریق

شرح این را گفتمی من از مری   لیک ترسم تا نلغزد خاطری

نکته ها چون تیغ پولادست تیز   گرنداری تو سپر، واپس گریز

We were simple and of one substance all,
We were all without head and foot in the beyond.
We were one substance like the sun,
We were without knots and pure like water.
When that pure Light took form,
It became number like the shadows of a niched battlement.
Tear down the niched battlement with the mangonel,
So that differences will disappear from within this squadron.
I would have this matter with diligence explained,
But I fear lest some minds might stumble.
Points here involved are like the blade of steel sharp,
If thou dost not have a shield, then turn back and flee!

Book I, v. 684-695

رو، بمعنـی کـوش ای صـورت پرسـت   ز آنـک معنی بـر تـن صـورت پرسـت

همنشـــین اهـــل معنـــی بـــاش، تـــا   هـــم عطـــا یـــابی و هـــم باشـــی فتـــی

VII

Go seek spiritual reality, o worshipper of form,
For spiritual reality is the wing of the body of form.
Become companion of people of spiritual reality,
So that thou wilt both receive the gift of Heaven and be chivalrous.

Book I, v. 714-715

مهـــر پاکـــان در میـــان جـــان نشـــان		دل مـــده الا بـــه مهـــر دلخوشـــان

کـــوی نومیـــدی مـــرو، اومیدهاســـت		ســـوی تـــاریکی مـــرو، خورشـــید هاســـت

دل تـــو را در کـــوی اهـــل دل کشـــد		تـــن تـــرا در حـــبس آب و گـــل کشـــد

هـــین! غـــذای دل بـــده از هـــم دلـــی		رو، بجـــو اقبـــال را از مقبلـــی

VIII

Plant the love of the pure within thy spirit,
And give not thy heart save to the love of them
whose hearts are content.
Go not to the quarter of despair for there is hope,
Go not towards darkness for there are suns.
The heart will drag thee to the abode of the people of the heart,
The body will drag thee to the prison of water and clay.
Oh! Feed thy heart with the food from a heart in accord,
Go, seek spiritual advancement from one already advanced.

Book I, v. 27-30

هـــم زبـــانی، خویشـــی و پیوندیســـت		مـــرد بـــا نامحرمـــان چـــون بندیســـت

ای بســـا هنـــدو و تـــرک هـــم زبـــان		ای بســـا دو تـــرک چـــون بیگانگـــان

پـس زبـان محرمـی ، خـود دیگرسـت		هـــم دلـــی از هـــم زبـــانی بهتـــر ســـت

غیرنطـــق و غیـــر ایمـــان و ســـجل		صـــد هـــزاران ترجمـــان خیـــزد زدل

IX

Having the same tongue is kinship and affinity,
With those with whom no intimacy exists, a man is as if in prison.
There are many Hindus and Turks with the same tongue,
And oh, many a pair of Turks, strangers to each other.
Hence the tongue of intimacy is something else,
It is better to be of one heart than of one tongue.
Without speech, without oath, without register,
A hundred thousand interpreters from the heart arise.

Book I, v. 1213-1216

با دوعالم، عشق را بیگانگی　　اندر و هفتاد و دو دیوانگی

سخت پنهانست و پیدا حیرتش　　جان سلطانان جان در حسرتش

غیر هفتاد و دو ملت کیش او　　تخت شاهان تخته بندی پیش او

مطرب عشق این زند وقت سماع　　بندگی بند و خداوندی صداع

پس چه باشد عشق؟ دریای عدم　　در شکسته عقل را آنجا قدم

بندگی و سلطنت معلوم شد　　زین دو پرده، عاشقی مکتوم شد

کاشکی، هستی زبانی داشتی!　　تا زهستان پرده ها برداشتی

هرچ گویی ای دم هستی از آن　　پردهٔ دیگر برو بستی ، بدان !

X

Love is to the two worlds a stranger,
Within it are seventy-two madnesses.
It is deeply hidden, its bewilderment manifest,
The soul of the kings of the soul in grief of it.
Its religion is other than that of the seventy-two creeds,
Before it the throne of kings is but a wooden boarding.
At the spiritual concert Love's minstrel this strain plays:
Servitude is bondage and lordship headache.
What then is Love? The sea of non-existence,
There the foot of reason does break.
Servitude and kingship have become known,
But behind their veil, Love has become concealed.
If only Existence had a tongue,
So that it could lift the veils from existing things.
O breath of Existence, whatever sayest thou of it,
Through those words another veil to it thou dost add.

Book III, v. 4722-4729

خــود خردآنســـت کـــو از حـــق چریـــد نـــه خـــرد کـــآنرا عطـــارد آوریـــد

پـــیش بینـــی ایـــن خـــرد تـــا گـــور بـــود و آن صـــاحب دل بـــه نفـــخ صـــور بـــود

ایـــن خـــرد از گـــور و خـــاکی نگـــذرد ویـــن قـــدم عرصـــه عجایـــب نســـپرد

زیـــن قـــدم ویـــن عقـــل، رو بیـــزار شـــو چشـــم غیبـــی جـــوی و بـــر خـــودار شـــو

XI

The intelligence pure is what is nourished by God,
Not that intelligence that was by Mercury the planet brought.
The foresight of this intelligence extends to the grave,
The intelligence of the spiritual extends to the Blast of the Trumpet.
This intelligence goes not beyond the grave and the earth,
It cannot set foot in the world of marvels.
From this step and this intelligence do become absolved,
Seek the eye that sees the invisible and from it benefit.

Book IV, v. 3311-3314

مـــی نـــماید صورت، ای صورت پرسـت کـــــان دو چشـــم مـــردهٔ او ناظرســـت

پـــیش چـــــشم نـــقش، مـــی آری ادب کـــوچـــرا پاســـم نمـــی دارد؟ عجـــب!

از چـــه بس بی پاسخست این نقش نیـک؟ کـــــه نـــمی گـــوید ســـلامم را علیـک

مـــی نجـــنباند ســـر و سبـلت ز جـــود پاس آن که کـردمش مـن صـد سجـــود

حـــق اگـر چـــه ســـر نـــجنباند بـــرون پـــاس آن ذوقـــی دهـــد درانـــدرون

کـــه دو صــــد جنبیـــدن ســـر ارزد آن ســـر چنـــین جنبانـد آخـر عقـــل و جـان

عـــقل راخـــدمـــت کـــنی در اجـــتهـاد پـــاس عـــقل آنـــست کافزایـد رشـــاد

XII

O worshipper of form, form does appear,
As if its two dead eyes were looking.
Thou showest reverence before the eye of the image,
Asking in wonder why it responds to thee not.
Why is this beautiful image irresponsive,
And answers not my "peace be upon thee" with "upon thee be peace"?
It moves not its head and moustache in generosity,
In response to a hundred prostrations I made before it.
The Divine Truth, although It moveth not Its head outwardly,
In response It bestoweth a spiritual delight within,
That is worth two hundred noddings of the head.
If thou servest the intellect with exertion,
The response of the intellect is to increase thy guidance.

حق نجنباند بظاهر سر تو را   لیک سازد بر سران سرور تو را

مر تو را چیزی دهد یزدان نهان   که سجود تو کننداهل جهان

آنچنانکه داد سنگی را هنر   تا عزیزخلق شد یعنی که زر

قطرهٔ آبی بیابد لطف حق   گوهری گردد، برد از زر سبق

جسم خاکست و چو حق تا بیش داد   در جهان گیری چو مه شد اوستاد

هین ! طلسمست این و نقش مرده است   احمقانرا چشمش از ره برده است

Outwardly, the Divine Truth doth not nod Its head to thee,
But It maketh thee the head of the heads of the world.
God bestoweth upon thee something in secret,
That makes the people of the world before thee bow.
In the same way that He gave a stone a virtue,
Which made it become dear to the world, that is, gold.
If a drop of water gains God's favor,
It becomes a pearl, outperforming gold.
The body is dust but when God sheddeth upon it a divine spark,
It became a master in conquering the world like the moon.
Beware! This world is a talisman and a dead image,
Its eye has led the fools astray from the Path.

Book IV, v. 3481-3494

کار دوزخ می کنی در خوردنی — بهر او خود را تو فربه می کنی

کار خود کن، روزی حکمت بچر — تا شود فربه دل با کر وفر

خوردن تن، مانع این خوردنست — جان چو بازرگان و تن چون ره زنست

شمع تاجر آنگهست افروخته — که بود ره زن چو هیزم سوخته

که توآن هوشی و باقی هوش پوش — خویشتن را گم مکن، یاوه مکوش

دانک هر شهوت چو خمرست و چو بنگ — پردهٔ هوشست و عاقل زوست دنگ

خمر تنها نیست سرمستی هوش — هر چه شهوانیست بندد چشم و گوش

XIII

In eating thou art doing the work of Hell,
For its sake thyself fattening.
Do thine own work, feed on wisdom's daily bread,
That thy heart may become mighty, strong and beautiful.
The eating of the body is an obstacle to this eating,
The spirit is like a merchant and the body a robber.
The candle of the merchant burns at that moment,
When the robber is consumed by fire like firewood.
For thou art consciousness, the rest a mask hiding consciousness,
Lose not thyself, seek not what is in vain.
Know that every passion is like wine and hemp,
It is the veil of consciousness, stupefying the intelligent.
Wine is not the only cause of the drunkenness of consciousness,
Whatever has passionate nature
    closes the inner eye and shuts the inner ear.

Book IV, v. 3608-

بـر فلـک محمـودی ای خورشـید فـاش
بـر زمـین هـم تـا ابـد محمـود بـاش

تـا زمینـی بـا سـمایی بلنـد
یـک دل و یـک قبلـه و یـک خوشـوند

تفرقـه بـر خیـزد و شـرک ودوی
وحدتسـت انـدر وجـود معنـوی

چـون شناسـد جـان مـن، جـان تـرا
یـاد آرنـد اتحـاد مـاجری

موسـی و هـارون شـوند انـدر زمـین
مخـتلط، خـوش، همچـو شـیر و انگبـین

چـون شناسـد انـدک و منکـر شـود
منکـری اش پـردهٔ سـاتر شـود

XIV

O manifest Sun, Thou in Heaven art glorified,
Be Thou also glorified on earth unto time's end.
So that those on earth with the exalted celestial realm,
May in heart, in prayer's direction, in nature one become.
So that dissipation, polytheism and duality will be removed,
For there is only unity in spiritual existence.
When my spirit comes to recognize Thy Spirit,
They will remember that they were in the past united.
They will become on earth like Moses and Aaron,
Mingled sweetly like milk and honey.
But when my spirit recognizes Thy Spirit only slightly and denies it,
The very denial becomes a veil covering the Truth.

Book IV, v. 3828-3833

CPSIA information can be obtained at www.ICGtesting.com
Printed in the USA
BVOW08s1659280616

453783BV00001B/3/P

9 780962 998454